CHI 7/06

ALLEN COUNTY PUBLIC LIBRARY

ACPL ITEM
DISCARDED

P9-EEN-954

Why is Keiko Sick?

Stacia McKeever

illustrated by Ingrid Beyer

Master Books

A Division of New Leaf Publishing Group

First Printing: March 2006

Copyright © 2006 by Stacia McKeever. All rights reserved. No part of this book may be reproduced in any manner whatsoever without written permission of the publisher except in the case of brief quotations in articles and reviews.

Printed in China

For information write:
Master Books
P.O. Box 726
Green Forest, AR 72638

Please visit our website for other great titles:
www.masterbooks.net

ISBN-13: 978-0-89051-463-4
ISBN-10: 0-89051-463-1
Library of Congress Number: 2005936554

Keiko's card

DEDICATION

We are grateful to God for our parents,

Robert and Nancy Byers
&
Karel and Yvonne Beyer,

who faithfully instilled in us a desire to love
our Savior and His Word.

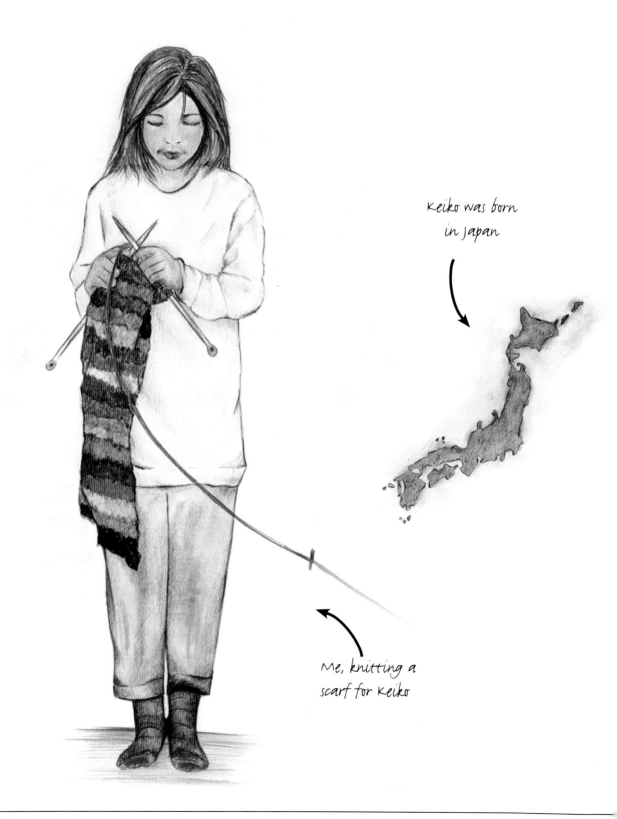

Keiko was born
in Japan

Me, knitting a
scarf for Keiko

My mom and I are knitting a scarf for Keiko. Keiko is my best friend. She was born in Japan, and her family moved to America when she was just a baby.

My mom

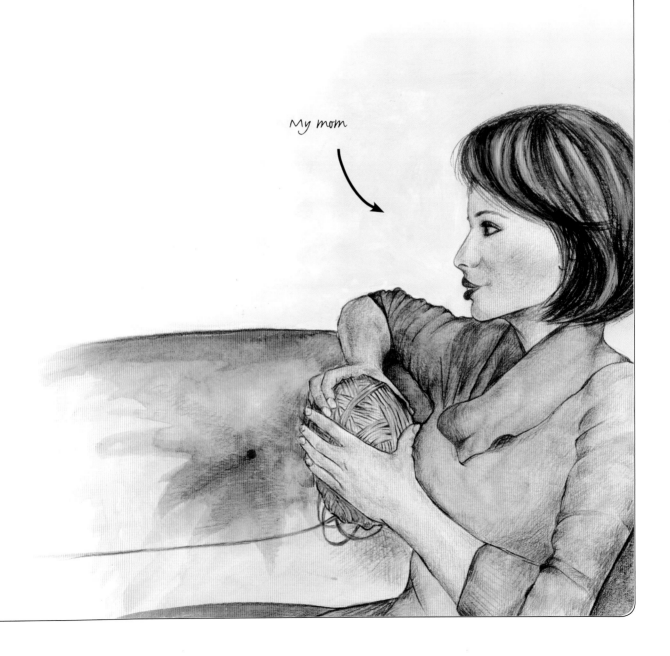

We do everything together. We like to ride our bikes up and down the street. Sometimes, Keiko teaches me Japanese words, like "自転車" which means "bike," and "道路" which means "street."

On rainy days, we like to curl up on our comfy couch and read books together. Our favorite stories are about dragons.

Keiko's mom says that a long time ago, the rulers of China used dragons to pull their chariots. Sometimes, Keiko and I wonder if dragons were really dinosaurs!

My best friend Keiko

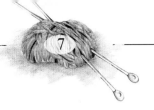

Keiko and I are learning to play the koto. The koto is a Japanese instrument that some say is shaped like a dragon. It has 13 strings. The names of the first ten strings are the numbers 1–10: ichi, ni, san, shi, go, roku, shichi/nana, hachi, kyu, and ju. The last three strings are to, i, and kin. Playing the koto helped me learn how to count to ten in Japanese!

The koto

One day, when I was getting ready to go to Keiko's house for our koto lesson, the telephone rang. When Mom hung up, she looked sad. She sat down on the couch and pulled me into her lap. Dad sat down beside her.

"I have something to tell you, Emily," she said. "Mrs. Qwan just called. She said Keiko is very sick. The doctor says Keiko has leukemia."

Mom told me that leukemia is a type of cancer. She said that means that the cells in Keiko's body aren't working right and they're making Keiko sick. That made me sad.

A picture of a dragon (or a dinosaur!) that Keiko and I like to read about.

Will Keiko die like Grandpa did?" I asked. "Well, eventually she will, Emily — eventually we all will. For now, though, the doctors think they'll be able to help her get better, but she'll need to stay in the hospital for a long time," Mom said. "Maybe when she's feeling better, we can go visit her. In the meantime, we can make some cards to send to her."

"Why does Keiko have to get sick?" I asked.

"Do you remember what we talked about last year when Grandpa died?" Dad asked.

"Yes, a little bit," I said.

Our family Bible

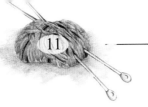

"Well, let me go get my Bible so I can explain this to you," he said. He got his Bible from the other room and said, "Remember how we talked about God creating the heavens and the earth about 6,000 years ago?" he asked me.

"Mmhmm," I said.

"Let's read what the Bible says about the very beginning." Dad opened his Bible, and pointed to Genesis 1.

My Dad

We read together, "God saw all that He had made, and behold, it was very good. And there was evening and there was morning, the sixth day.

"After God had created the plants and trees, and swimming and flying creatures, and land creatures and the first two people, He said that what He had created was 'very good.' It was perfect and complete — just the way He wanted it. The first two people. . . ."

"Adam and Eve?" I said.

"That's right. Adam and Eve were the very first people, and God had created them in His image — He created Adam from the dust of the ground, and Eve from Adam's side. He gave them a beautiful place to live, and gave Adam one rule to follow," Dad said. "Let's read about that rule."

Dad turned to Genesis 2, and I read, "From any tree of the garden you may eat freely; but from the tree of the knowledge of good and evil you shall not eat, for in the day that you eat from it you will surely die."

"God created Adam and Eve and all the animals perfectly — they never got sick with diseases like leukemia, and the animals never even thought about eating one another. They all ate the fruit and plants God had given them," Dad said. "But something happened to change all that."

"Instead of listening to the Creator and obeying His command, Adam sinned when he rebelled against God. Adam chose to eat from the Tree of the Knowledge of Good and Evil. When he did that, everything changed. The earth was no longer the perfect place God had created, and Adam and Eve were no longer the perfect people God had created."

God is holy, which means He is pure — He is without sin. Because He is holy, He must punish disobedience. So, God punished Adam and Eve."

Dad turned to Genesis 3, and read verse 19, ". . . By the sweat of your face you will eat bread, till you return to the ground, because from it you were taken; for you are dust, and to dust you shall return."

Dad said, "God sent Adam and Eve from the beautiful garden He had formed for them, so that they wouldn't eat from the Tree of Life and live forever as sinners.

"Because Adam sinned, each of Adam's children was born a sinner, and each of us sins. Because of that sin, we all die, and as part of that, we get sick. Some people develop cancer, like Keiko. Others have heart problems, like Grandpa. Some people can't see or hear."

A ribbon Keiko gave me to wear to make people aware of leukemia

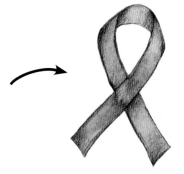

G od also placed a curse on the ground," Dad said, "causing it to grow thorns and thistles, and making it difficult for people to make a living off the ground. After Adam's sin, even the animals were changed and began to die — some began to eat each other, like that cat that we saw kill a bird the other day. It's all part of the world that we now live in."

Dad turned to Romans 8 and we read, "For we know that the whole creation groans and suffers the pains of childbirth together until now.

"In fact," Dad continued, "The reason we wear clothes is because of sin in the world. After Adam and Eve disobeyed, they knew they had done wrong and they tried to cover up what they had done by making clothes from plant leaves.

"But those clothes weren't able to cover their sin. Instead, God had to kill an animal to make clothes for them — that was the very first time anything died in that once-perfect place."

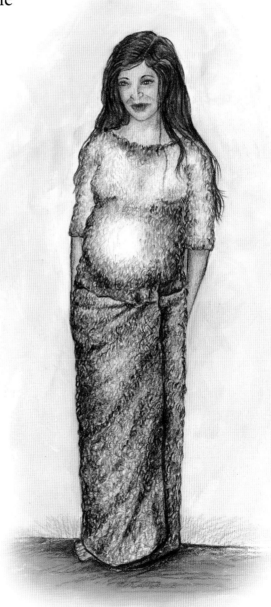

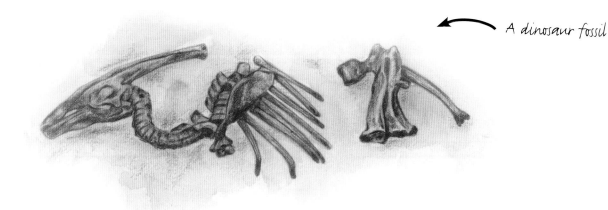

A dinosaur fossil

Think for a minute about the sad things that happen — like Grandpa dying or Keiko getting sick . . ."

"What about the earthquakes where Aunt Lyn lives, Daddy?" I said. "Yes, sweetie, even the earthquakes and tsunamis, and the wars that you've heard Mom and I talk about . . .

My grandpa

A local flood in my neighborhood two years ago

"All these are terrible and sad things. But I want you to understand that they are not God's fault."

We read Romans 5, "Therefore, just as through one man sin entered into the world, and death through sin, and so death spread to all men, because all sinned."

Dad said, "When each of us sins, we're actually saying that we don't want God in our lives. So, with these terrible things, we experience a little bit of what it is like to not have Him in our lives."

"But I don't want to be without God, Daddy," I said.

"Well, I have good news for you, Emily," Dad said. "God had a plan for His creation."

Dad pointed to Genesis 3:15, "And I will put hatred between you and the woman, and between your seed and her seed; he shall bruise you on the head, and you shall bruise him on the heel." Dad said that meant that God promised to one day send someone who would save His people from their sins.

"And 4,000 years after that first promise, at the exact time God had planned, the Creator God came to earth as a tiny baby." Dad turned to Galatians 4 and we read, "But when the fullness of the time came, God sent forth His Son, born of a woman."

"The Bible tells us that Jesus grew and obeyed His parents, and God. Unlike Adam, and the rest of us who disobey, Jesus never disobeyed — He never sinned. Yet, according to the plan of God, Jesus was put to death. Not for His own sins, but for ours."

Then Dad turned to Romans 5 and read, "But God demonstrates His own love toward us, in that while we were yet sinners, Christ died for us.

"You see, Emily, the Bible tells us that God loves His children and has a gift for them — the gift of eternal life. God has a special book called the Lamb's Book of Life. He's written the names of all those who have eternal life in there. The Bible tells us that we can know for certain that our names are there. Let's look at Romans 10."

"That if you confess with your mouth, 'Jesus is Lord,' and believe in your heart that God raised him from the dead, you will be saved," we read.

oes all this make sense to you, Emily? Do you have any questions?" Dad asked.

"Yes, Daddy, I understand," I said.

"That was a long answer, but did I answer your question about why Keiko is sick?" Dad asked.

I thought about how God created Adam and Eve in their perfect garden, and how they disobeyed and everything changed, and about how I sometimes disobey my parents.

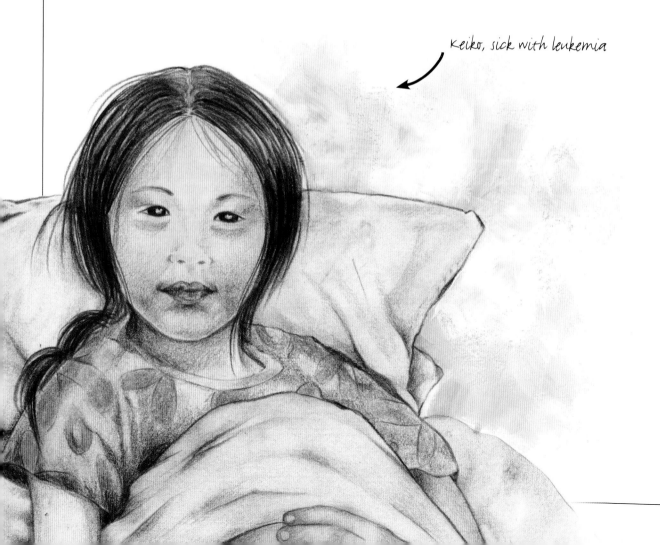

Keiko, sick with leukemia

Then I thought about how because of all our sin, Keiko has cancer. It made me sad.

"Yes, Daddy. Keiko is sick because of sin in the world," I said.

"That's right, Emily," he said. "Although, I want you to understand that it's not necessarily because of any particular sin that you or I have committed.

"And, remember that God loves the world so much that He is offering eternal life through Jesus to those who will receive it, even though we've done nothing to deserve this wonderful gift."

"How can I help Keiko get better?" I asked.

"Well, we can pray that the Lord would be pleased to heal Keiko," Dad said.

"Do you think He will make Keiko better?" I asked.

"I don't know, Emily. He may choose to make her better, but He also may choose to heal Keiko in a different way from what we might want Him to. If Keiko should die, like Grandpa did last year, and she is a Christian like Grandpa was, then she'll have the best healing! She would be with God in heaven where no one is sick, or has cancer," Dad said.

Me, making a card for Keiko

Dear Keiko I hope you'll Get well soon. your

"Whatever happens, we know that God is good and His ways are perfect. He causes everything to work together for good to those who love Him," Mom said.

She said, "The Bible says that God has promised to create a new heaven and earth for His children. In our world, death is an enemy, but in that place, there will be no more death or sickness. The new heaven and earth will be just like this current earth was in the beginning — a 'very good' place!

"And, although Keiko is too sick for us to visit now, we can make some cards to send to her. And I'll teach you how to knit so that you can knit a scarf as a present for Keiko," Mom said.

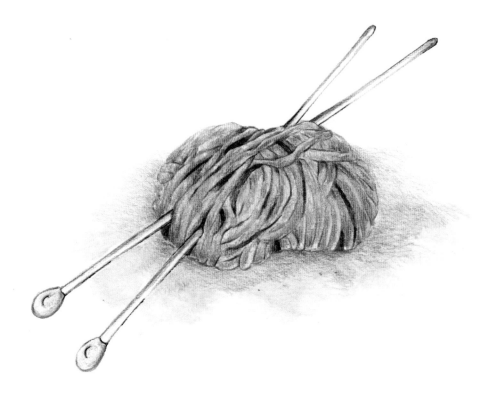

So that's why we're knitting a scarf for Keiko. I'm going to give it to her tomorrow, when she comes home from the hospital.

Keiko's card

Me, starting Keiko's scarf

I can't wait to teach Keiko how to knit, too! And I hope we get to start playing the koto together again, like we did before Keiko got sick.

keiko's scarf

THINGS TO DO AND TALK ABOUT TOGETHER…

1. Read through Genesis 1–3 together.

2. What does "holy" mean? Read the following verses that talk about the holiness of God: 1 Samuel 1:1–2; Psalm 30:4; Psalm 77:12–14; Psalm 99:5; Isaiah 6:3; Revelation 4:8. What other verses can you find? Choose one or two to memorize.

3. How did God describe His original creation? (Read Genesis 1:29–30.) What do you imagine a "very good" world would look like? Draw a picture of what you're imagining.

4. What did God give Adam and Eve and the animals to eat in the very beginning? (Read Genesis 1:29–30.) What are your favorite fruits and veggies? Today, we like to eat things other than fruits and vegetables. Why are we allowed to do this? (Look up Genesis 9:1–3.)

5. What happened to change the "very good" world into the sad world we see today? (Read Genesis 3.) Make a list of things that changed after Adam disobeyed, according to Genesis 3. Draw pictures (or find some in old magazines) that illustrate the points in your list.

6. What things aren't "very good" today? What things make you sad? Write a story about something that makes you sad.

7. Do you know anyone who has cancer or is sick? What could you do for them?

(Maybe you could make them a card or learn how to knit something for them, like Emily did for Keiko!)

8. What is "sin"? What kinds of things do we do that "miss the mark" of God's perfect standard (holiness)? What did God tell Adam was the punishment for sin? (Look up Genesis 2:17; Genesis 3:19, 22–24; Romans 6:23.)

9. Some people say that death is a "natural" part of the world today — that it has been around since the very beginning of time. But what does the Bible say about death? (Read Romans 5:12; 1 Corinthians 15:26, 54–57.) Who gives us victory over death?

10. What did God do to provide a covering for Adam and Eve's disobedience? (Read Genesis 3:21.) At least one animal had to die in order for God to make clothes for Adam and Eve. What does the Bible say about how sins are to be covered? (Look up Hebrews 9:22; Hebrews 10:4; 1 Peter 3:18.) Who died on the Cross to take away the sin of the world? (Read John 1:29.)

11. Our sin separates us from our Holy Creator. What gift does He offer to us? (Look up Romans 6:23 and Ephesians 2:8–9.) How do we receive this gift? (Read John 3:16; John 6:39–40; John 17:1–3; Romans 10:9–10; 1 John 5:10–13.) What happens to those who do not receive this gift? (Read Matthew 25:46; John 3:36; John 5:24.)

12. Read about the Lamb's Book of Life. (Look up Philippians 4:3; Revelation 3:5; Revelation 20:11–13; Revelation 20:15; Revelation 21:27.) Do you know for certain that your name is written there?

13. What will the new heaven and Earth be like? (See Revelation 21–22.) List the ways the new heaven and Earth will be different from our current world. Draw a picture of what you think the "Tree of Life" might look like.

14. Read through the following verses: Romans 5:8; Romans 8:20–22, 28; Romans 10:9–10; Galatians 4:4. Choose one or two verses to memorize.

15. Locate China and Japan on a map. Learn how to say and write "hello" in Japanese. Find out more about the koto.

16. Emily and Keiko think that dragons could have actually been dinosaurs! What do you think? Find out more about dragon legends.

17. Emily's father said God created the world about 6,000 years ago. Other people say it is millions of years old! What does the Bible teach about how old the earth is? (See www.AnswersInGenesis.org/Ussher.)

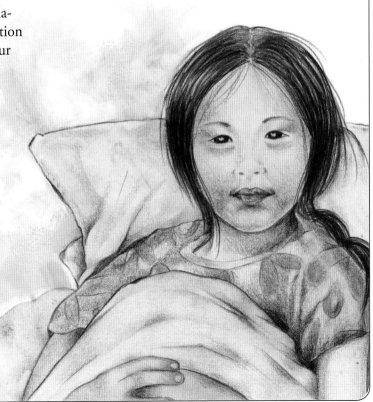

Also Available . . .

A is for Adam

*Ken & Mally Ham
& Dan Lietha*

Children will delight in the colorful illustrations and rhymes herein that teach about creation and the gospel. This three-part family book is an ABC book, a coloring book, and a home-devotional teaching book.

Dinosaurs of Eden

*Ken Ham &
Earl & Bonita Snellenberger*

A fun way for teens to learn about dinosaurs throughout history, from the Garden of Eden to the Flood to Job. This book also explores the possibility that dinosaurs could still be around today. Full-color illustrations on each page highlight over 40 species of dinosaurs.

Preschool
0-89051-207-8 • 120 pages • Hardcover • Color interior
$15.99

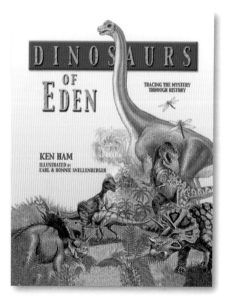

Science & Faith 8-HS
0-89051-340-6 • 64 pages • Hardcover • Color interior
$13.99

Available at Christian Bookstores Nationwide!